ANIMALS OF THE ARCTIC TUNDRA POLAR REGION WILDLIFE

Arctic tundra is found almost entirely in the Northern Hemisphere.

The polar bear are the world's largest land predators. Polar bears spend most of their time at sea. They primarily eat seals.

Arctic fox is small animal that can reach 26 inches in length. Their hearing is so good that they can locate the exact position of their prey under the snow.

Caribou is a
large mammal.
It can reach 240
to 700 pounds in
weight. Caribou
releases special
scent when faced
with danger, it
informs other
caribous about
near danger.

Arctic hares
are the largest
hares. Arctic
hares have black
eyelashes that
protect their
eyes from the
sun's glare, just
like sunglasses.

Snowy owls hunt actively during both day and night and are thus called, diurnal. They stay warm as their feathers do not have any pigments which leaves more room for air.

Musk oxen are herbivores. These arctic animals have thick hair that grows 2 feet long and almost touches the ground. They can weigh as much as 850 pounds.

Arctic Wolves live in very cold climates sometimes reaching -30 degrees. Arctic Wolves have two layers of very white fur to protect them against the cold temperatures.